Editor
Eric Migliaccio

Managing Editor
Ina Massler Levin, M.A.

Editor-in-Chief
Sharon Coan, M.S. Ed.

Illustrator
Alexandra Artigas

Cover Artist
Barb Lorseyedi

Art Coordinator
Kevin Barnes

Art Director
CJae Froshay

Imaging
Craig Gunnell

Product Manager
Phil Garcia

Publisher
Mary D. Smith, M.S. Ed.

Grades K–2

REPRODUCIBLE LITTLE BOOKS
for
Sight Words

I can see

green

big

purple

Author

Patricia Tilton, M.A. Ed.

Teacher Created Resources, Inc.
6421 Industry Way
Westminster, CA 92683
www.teachercreated.com
ISBN 13: 978-0-7439-3225-7
ISBN 10: 0-7439-3225-0
©2004 Teacher Created Resources, Inc
Reprinted, 2006
Made in U.S.A.

Table of Contents

Introduction

What Are High-Frequency Words?

In the English language, there are over 100 words that appear with the highest occurrence in written text. These words are known as *high-frequency words*.

Good readers know these high-frequency words automatically, or by "sight." This enables them to read with fluency and better comprehend text because every word does not need to be decoded. A beginning reader who must focus on decoding every word is unable to devote enough attention to comprehension and fluency. Good teachers give students the strategies and techniques necessary to decode text, including the ability to recognize high-frequency words as sight words.

Introduction (cont.)

What Are High-Frequency Words? (cont.)

The problem with high-frequency words is that they are usually meaningless abstract words that may have irregular spellings and pronunciations. Many high-frequency words are connecting words and have little meaning out of context (for example, *have, of, are, said*). Using high-frequency words to create a bank of sight words and using the sight words in context enables students to do the following:

1. Establish a bank of sight words
2. Transfer these sight words to text
3. Reread sight-word text to accelerate fluency
4. Develop a positive self-image by experiencing success

The word list and accompanying stories were created to be used as part of a literacy program to stress recognition of high-frequency words and to develop fluency. Their purpose is not to take the place of a balanced literacy program, but to be included in any program in order to help students develop into proficient readers.

Purpose of *Reproducible Little Books for Sight Words*

Reading is an interactive process and word-recognition skills, fluency, and self-esteem are all an interwoven part of that process. This book builds success for the beginning reader by using high-frequency words to create a bank of sight words that are automatically recognized. By also developing and improving fluency through the use of rereading familiar texts, a successful experience is created and students see themselves as readers. Providing students with a large sight-word vocabulary and developing fluency meet National Education Standards, which state "students need to understand level appropriate sight words (e.g., high frequency words such as *said, was, where*)" and read "familiar stories, poems and passages with fluency." (Used with permission from McREL. Copyright 2000 McREL, Mid-continent Research for Education and Learning. Telephone: 303-337-0990. Web site: *www.mcrel.org*)

Word-Recognition Skills

The word lists and stories in this book provide an opportunity for a beginning reader to improve word-recognition skills by building a bank of quickly and automatically recognizable sight words. Students are given a list of words, which then appear in a controlled vocabulary story. The lists are sequential and all previous lists are scaffolded into the new stories. An index of the sight words that are used in the stories is provided on page 176.

Fluency

Word recognition has also been shown to strengthen and improve fluency. Readers who do not have to stop and decode every word read with more fluidity and expression.

Self-Esteem

Experiencing success is crucial to the beginning reader, and the word lists and stories provide an environment for success. Controlling the vocabulary allows students to have a successful reading experience by minimizing frustration and encouraging repetitive usage both in isolation and in context.

How to Use the Word Lists

Each word-list unit contains a list of high-frequency words that are to be learned as sight words. Each section provides opportunities to practice the words with in-class activities and homework, which scaffolds learning. Assessment is also included with two running records provided for each section. When and how often to use the word lists depends on the ability of the students. Here are a few suggestions:

> ➤ Each section can be done in one week, or the flash cards can be learned one week and stories practiced the following week.

> ➤ The word lists can also be used as spelling words when they are introduced; or after finishing the 12 sections, review the words by using them for spelling.

Here is a description of each of the six types of activities included in each word-list unit:

1. Flash Cards

The flash card page is sent home and practiced. Index cards can also be used to make the flash cards. The cards can be kept in an envelope or plastic baggie, or consider putting them on a ring and attaching them to the child's backpack. Access to the words can make practice easier when waiting on the playground or riding the bus.

2. Homework Stories

The four stories are sent home at the beginning of each unit as or with homework so the students may practice them at home. If the student is an English Language Learner or has no one at home to help, consider tape-recording the stories.

3. Word-List Story Books

Fold the book pages in half and staple together with a construction paper cover. The books can be kept at the student's desk and practiced when other work is finished. Consider using a baggie to collect the book(s) and hang them from the students' desks with a magnetic or adhesive hook to provide easy access for familiar reading.

4. Library Box

Each story is printed individually for use in the classroom library. Providing copies of the stories in the classroom library gives the students another opportunity to practice the sight words and reread for fluency. Consider coloring the pictures, mounting them on construction paper, and laminating them.

5. Cut-Up Sentences

Several sentences are pulled from the stories to be used as further practice in a small group or individually. Each child cuts up one sentence, mixes the words, and "rewrites" the sentence by manipulating the pieces. For easy management, consider using library pockets with the sentence written on the front and the cut-up words kept inside.

6. Running Records

Each section contains two running records. They can be used to assess whether a student has mastered the words and text. Consider holding back one story and using the running record to assess unfamiliar text.

Definitions of Terms Used

Comprehension
- getting meaning from text, understanding what is read

Controlled Vocabulary
- words in the text are purposely selected to reinforce known words and introduce new words

Cross-Checking
- using two or more strategies together when decoding text

Decode
- analyze unknown words using a variety of strategies

Fluency
- combination of word recognition and speed, making reading "sound like talking"

High-Frequency Words
- words that appear more frequently than most others in spoken or written language and should generally be learned as "sight words"

Meaning Cueing System
- using pictures and content to decode unknown words

Running Record
- an assessment used to measure reading accuracy

Running Words
- the number of words read during the taking of a running record

Sight Words
- words that are immediately recognized in their entirety and do not require word analysis for identification

Strategies
- techniques and methods used in decoding text

Visual Cueing System
- using the sound/symbol relationship to decode unknown words

Word Bank
- all the written words a students recognizes automatically

How to Use Running Records

A *running record* is an assessment of text reading to determine which strategies a student is using effectively. For the purposes of this book, the running records assess whether or not a student recognizes sight words in context.

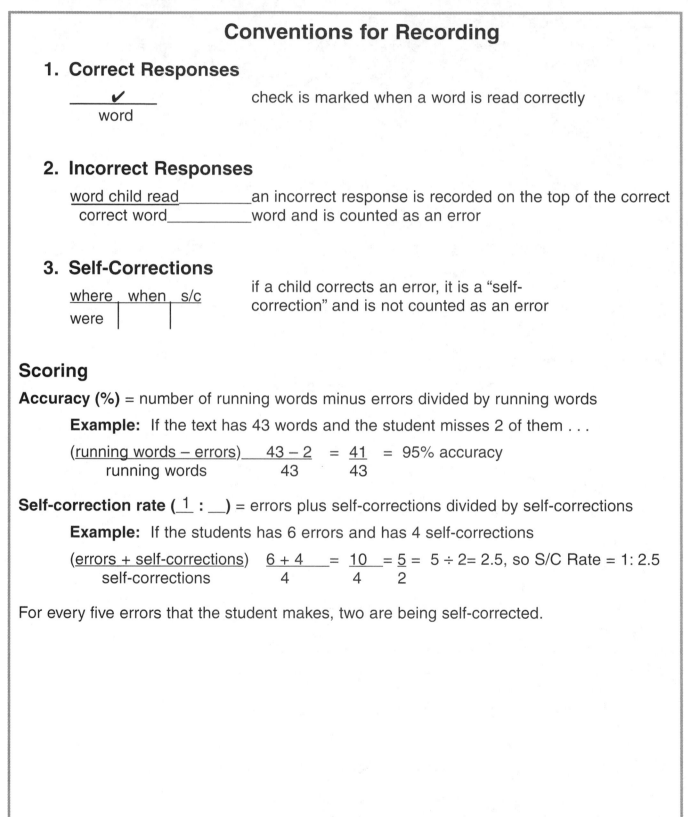

Conventions for Recording

1. Correct Responses

✔
word

check is marked when a word is read correctly

2. Incorrect Responses

word child read
correct word

an incorrect response is recorded on the top of the correct word and is counted as an error

3. Self-Corrections

where when s/c
were

if a child corrects an error, it is a "self-correction" and is not counted as an error

Scoring

Accuracy (%) = number of running words minus errors divided by running words

   Example: If the text has 43 words and the student misses 2 of them . . .

   $$\frac{\text{running words} - \text{errors}}{\text{running words}} \quad \frac{43-2}{43} = \frac{41}{43} = 95\% \text{ accuracy}$$

Self-correction rate (_1_ : __) = errors plus self-corrections divided by self-corrections

   Example: If the students has 6 errors and has 4 self-corrections

   $$\frac{\text{errors} + \text{self-corrections}}{\text{self-corrections}} \quad \frac{6+4}{4} = \frac{10}{4} = \frac{5}{2} = 5 \div 2 = 2.5, \text{ so S/C Rate} = 1:2.5$$

For every five errors that the student makes, two are being self-corrected.

Alphabetical Listing of Sight Words

Aa	List When Word Introduced
a	4
after	7
all	9
am	7
and	2
are	9
at	3
away	8

Bb

been	12
big	4
black	4
blue	1
boy	5
but	8
by	8

Cc

came	12
can	2
come	3

Dd

did	11
do	4
down	6

Ee

eat	8

Ff

fast	11
for	7
friend	9
funny	6

Gg	List When Word Introduced
get	7
go	2
good	9
got	11
green	1

Hh

has	6
have	7
he	4
help	5
here	3
home	6

Ii

I	1
in	6
is	4
it	5

Jj

jump	3

Ll

like	1
little	5
look	3

Mm

made	12
make	10
many	12
me	2
my	5

Nn	List When Word Introduced
new	11
not	6

Oo

of	12
on	5
one	9
orange	1
out	10
over	12

Pp

play	2
please	7
purple	4
put	10

Rr

ran	8
red	1
ride	11
run	6

Ss

said	5
saw	8
see	2
she	7
so	10
some	7

Tt	List When Word Introduced
take	11
tell	10
the	1
they	9
this	6
to	2
today	10

Uu

up	3
us	12
use	10

Vv

very	11

Ww

want	5
was	11
we	2
went	9
were	12
what	10
when	8
where	9
will	3
with	4

Yy

yellow	1
yes	8
you	3

Word List	Times used in stories
1. I	16
2. like	16
3. the	16
4. yellow	4
5. red	3
6. green	2
7. blue	2
8. orange	3

Times Word Is Used in *Each* Story

	"The Butterfly"	"The Flower"	"The Bird"	"The Dog"
1. I	4	4	4	4
2. like	4	4	4	4
3. the	4	4	4	4
4. yellow	1	1	1	1
5. red	0	1	1	1
6. green	1	1	0	0
7. blue	1	0	0	1
8. orange	1	1	1	0

Reading Strategies to Introduce

- *Using Known Words*—recognizing words known in isolation in the context of a story

- *Checking Pictures for Meaning*—decoding an unknown word using the picture for clues (student must look at a picture in a story to decode *butterfly*, *flower*, *bird*, and *dog*; pictures may be color coded to provide additional support for color words)

- *1:1 Correspondence*—using a finger to point to each word as it is being spoken (also called *tracking*)

Word List #1: Sight-Word Stories

Story #1 — The Butterfly

I like the blue butterfly.

I like the orange butterfly.

I like the green butterfly.

I like the yellow butterfly.

(20 running words)

Story #2 — The Flower

I like the red flower.

I like the orange flower.

I like the green flower.

I like the yellow flower.

(20 running words)

Story #3 — The Bird

I like the red bird.

I like the yellow bird.

I like the orange bird.

I like the bird.

(19 running words)

Story #4 — The Dog

I like the dog.

I like the yellow dog.

I like the red dog.

I like the blue dog.

(19 running words)

Word List #1: Flash Cards

I	like
the	yellow
red	green
orange	blue

Word List #1: Homework

The Butterfly

I like the blue butterfly.

I like the orange butterfly.

I like the green butterfly.

I like the yellow butterfly.

The Flower

I like the red flower.

I like the orange flower.

I like the green flower.

I like the yellow flower.

The Bird

I like the red bird.

I like the yellow bird.

I like the orange bird.

I like the bird.

The Dog

I like the dog.

I like the yellow dog.

I like the red dog.

I like the blue dog.

Word List #1: Story Books

The Flower

I like the red flower.

I like the orange flower.

I like the green flower.

I like the yellow flower.

The Butterfly

I like the blue butterfly.

I like the orange butterfly.

I like the green butterfly.

I like the yellow butterfly.

Word List #1: Story Books

The Dog

I like the dog.

I like the yellow dog.

I like the red dog.

I like the blue dog.

The Bird

I like the red bird.

I like the yellow bird.

I like the orange bird.

I like the bird.

Word List #1: Library Box

The Butterfly

I like the blue butterfly.

I like the orange butterfly.

I like the green butterfly.

I like the yellow butterfly.

Word List #1: Library Box

The Dog

I like the dog.

I like the yellow dog.

I like the red dog.

I like the blue dog.

Word List #1: Library Box

The Flower

I like the red flower.

I like the orange flower.

I like the green flower.

I like the yellow flower.

Word List #1: Library Box

The Bird

I like the red bird.

I like the yellow bird.

I like the orange bird.

I like the bird.

Word List #1: Cut-Up Sentences

I like the yellow	the like	I like
	I	I
I	butterfly.	bird.
		red

Word List #1: Cut-Up Sentences

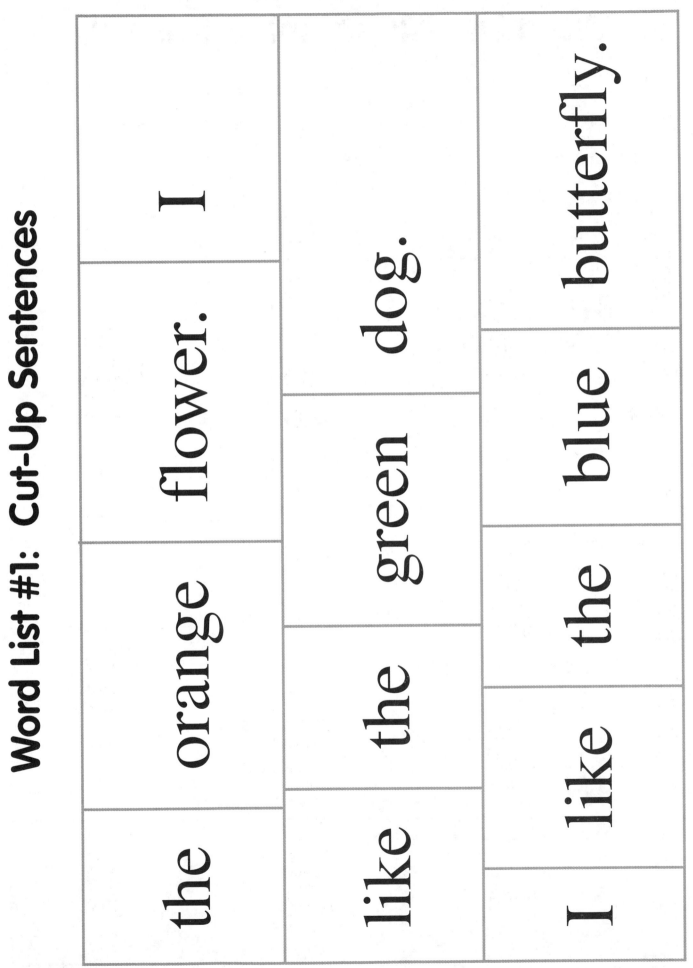

I	flower.	orange	the
dog.	green	the	like
butterfly.	blue	the.	like	I

Word List #1: Running Records

Name: _____   _____ % Accuracy

Date: _____   1: _____ S/C Ratio

"The Dog"

(*19 Running Words*)	errors	self-corrections
I like the dog. I like the yellow dog. I like the red dog. I like the blue dog.		
Totals:		

Running Words – Errors = % of Accuracy   19 – _____ = _____ % Accuracy
  Running Words

Errors + Self-Corrections (S/C) = S/C Rate   _____ + _____ = _1 : ____ S/C Rate
  Self-Corrections

Accuracy Levels
100% – 94% = easy
94% – 90% = instructional
below 90% = frustration

Comments and Observations:

Word List #1: Running Records

Name: _____   _____ % Accuracy

Date: _____   1: _____ S/C Ratio

"The Bird"

(19 Running Words)	errors	self-corrections
I like the red bird. I like the yellow bird. I like the orange bird. I like the bird.		
Totals:		

Running Words – Errors = % of Accuracy   19 – _____ = _____ % Accuracy
    Running Words

Errors + Self-Corrections (S/C) = S/C Rate   _____ + _____ = __1 :___ S/C Rate
    Self-Corrections

> **Accuracy Levels**
> 100% – 94% = easy
> 94% – 90% = instructional
> below 90% = frustration

Comments and Observations:

Word List	Times used in stories
1. see	4
2. to	3
3. we	4
4. can	6
5. play	11
6. and	6
7. go	6
8. me	2

Times Word is Used In *Each* Story

	"The Blue Bird"	"I Like to Play"	"We Can Play"	"See Me Play"
1. see	2	0	0	2
2. to	0	1	1	1
3. we	0	0	4	0
4. can	0	2	3	1
5. play	0	4	2	5
6. and	0	1	3	2
7. go	0	0	5	1
8. me	0	0	0	2

Number of times words from Word List #1 are used → 15

Reading Strategies to Review

- Using Known Words
- Checking Pictures For Meaning
- 1:1 Correspondence

Reading Strategies to Introduce

Question mark (?)—recognizing the symbol and the change it causes in intonation and expression when reading

Word List #2: Sight-Word Stories

Story #1 — The Blue Bird

See the bird.

See the blue bird.

I like the blue bird.

(12 running words)

Story #2 — I Like to Play

I like to play.

I can play.

I can play and play.

(12 running words)

Story #3 — We Can Play

We can go.

We like to go and go.

We can go and play.

Can we go and play?

(19 running words)

Story #4 — See Me Play

I can play.

See me play.

I like to play and play.

See me go and play.

(17 running words)

Word List #2: Flash Cards

see	to
we	can
play	and
go	me

Word List #2: Homework

The Blue Bird

See the bird.

See the blue bird.

I like the blue bird.

I Like to Play

I like to play.

I can play.

I can play and play.

We Can Play

We can go.

We like to go and go.

We can go and play.

Can we go and play?

See Me Play

I can play.

See me play.

I like to play and play.

See me go and play.

Word List #2: Story Book

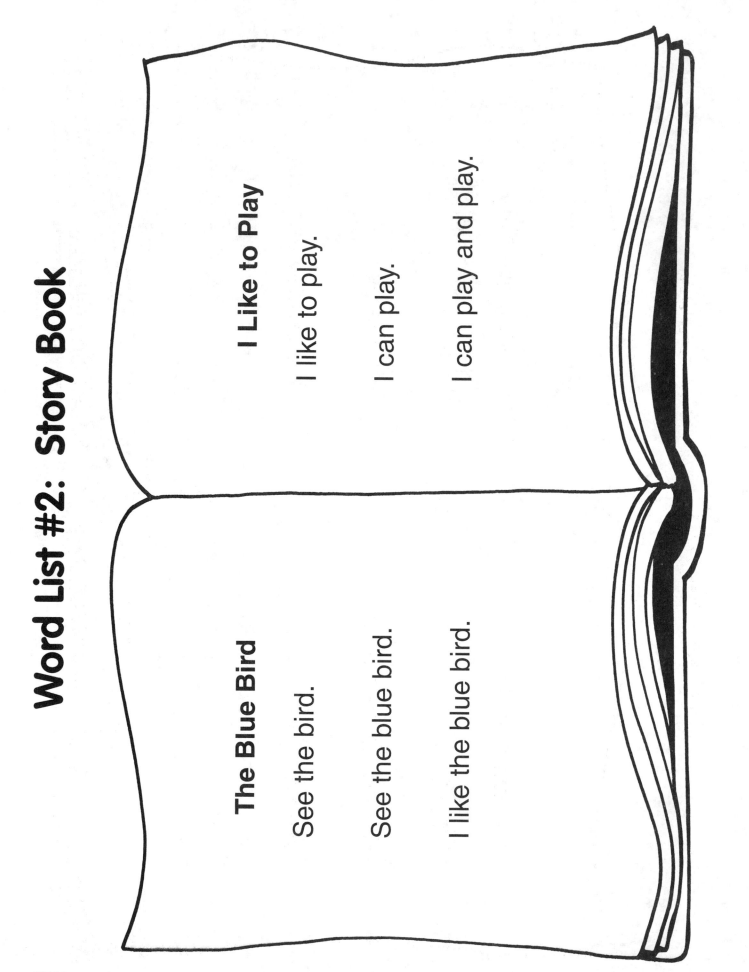

I Like to Play

I like to play.

I can play.

I can play and play.

The Blue Bird

See the bird.

See the blue bird.

I like the blue bird.

Word List #2: Story Book

See Me Play

I can play.

See me play.

I like to play and play.

See me go and play.

We Can Play

We can go.

We like to go and go.

We can go and play.

Can we go and play?

Word List #2: Library Box

The Blue Bird

See the bird.
See the blue bird.
I like the blue bird.

Word List #2: Library Box

I Like to Play

I like to play.
I can play.
I can play and play.

Word List #2: Library Box

We Can Play

We can go.
We like to go and go.
We can go and play.
Can we go and play?

Word List #2: Library Box

See Me Play

I can play.
See me play.
I like to play and play.
See me go and play.

Word List #2: Cut-Up Sentences

We	like	to	go	and	go.

See	me.	go	and	play.

Can	we	go	and	play?

Word List #2: Cut-Up Sentences

I	can	and	play.
I	like	to	play	and	play.
See	the	blue	bird.

Word List #2: Running Records

Name: _____   _____ % Accuracy

Date: _____   1: _____ S/C Ratio

"We Can Play"

(*19 Running Words*)	errors	self-corrections
We can go. We like to go and go. We can go and play. Can we go and play?		
Totals:		

<u>Running Words – Errors</u> = % of Accuracy
    Running Words

  _19_ – _____ = _____ % Accuracy

<u>Errors + Self-Corrections (S/C)</u> = S/C Rate
    Self-Corrections

  _____ + _____ = _1 :_____ S/C Rate

> **Accuracy Levels**
> 100% – 94% = easy
> 94% – 90% = instructional
> below 90% = frustration

> **Comments and Observations:**
>
>
>
>

Word List #2: Running Records

Name: _____   _____ % Accuracy

Date: _____   1: _____ S/C Ratio

"See Me Play"

(17 Running Words)	errors	self-corrections
I can play. See me play. I like to play and play. See me go and play.		
Totals:		

Running Words – Errors = % of Accuracy
    Running Words

17 – _____ = _____ % Accuracy

Errors + Self-Corrections (S/C) = S/C Rate
    Self-Corrections

_____ + _____ = 1 : ____ S/C Rate

Accuracy Levels

100% – 94% = easy

94% – 90% = instructional

below 90% = frustration

Comments and Observations:

Word List	Times used in stories
1. at	3
2. come	7
3. here	6
4. will	3
5. jump	3
6. up	3
7. look	5
8. you	4

Times Word Is Used in *Each* Story

	"Look At Me"	"Come Up Here"	"Jump"	"To the Zoo"
1. at	1	0	1	1
2. come	4	2	0	1
3. here	3	3	0	0
4. will	1	0	0	2
5. jump	0	0	3	0
6. up	0	3	0	0
7. look	2	0	2	1
8. you	2	0	1	1

Number of times words from Word Lists #1 and #2 are used → 40

Reading Strategies to Review

- Using Known Words
- Checking Pictures For Meaning
- 1:1 Correspondence
- Question Mark

Reading Strategies to Introduce

Exclamation Point (!)—recognizing the symbol and the change it causes in intonation and expression when reading

Word List #3: Sight-Word Stories

Story #1 — Look At Me

Look! Look at me.

Come here to me.

Come and see me.

You can come here.

Will you come here?

(*20 running words*)

Story #2 — Come Up Here

Come up here.

Come up here and see me.

I can see.

I can see up here.

(*17 running words*)

Story #3 — Jump

Look at me!

Look! I can jump.

Can you jump?

I like to jump.

(*12 running words*)

Story #4 — To the Zoo

I will go to the zoo.

I like the zoo.

I like to play at the zoo.

Look! I see the zoo.

Will you come to the zoo?

(*12 running words*)

Word List #3: Flash Cards

at	come
here	will
jump	up
look	you

Word List #3: Homework

Look At Me

Look! Look at me.

Come here to me.

Come and see me.

You can come here.
-
Will you come here?

Come Up Here

Come up here.

Come up here and see me.

I can see.

I can see up here.

Jump

Look at me!

Look! I can jump.

Can you jump?

I like to jump.

To the Zoo

I will go to the zoo.

I like the zoo.

I like to play at the zoo.

Look! I see the zoo.

Will you come to the zoo?

Word List #3: Story Books

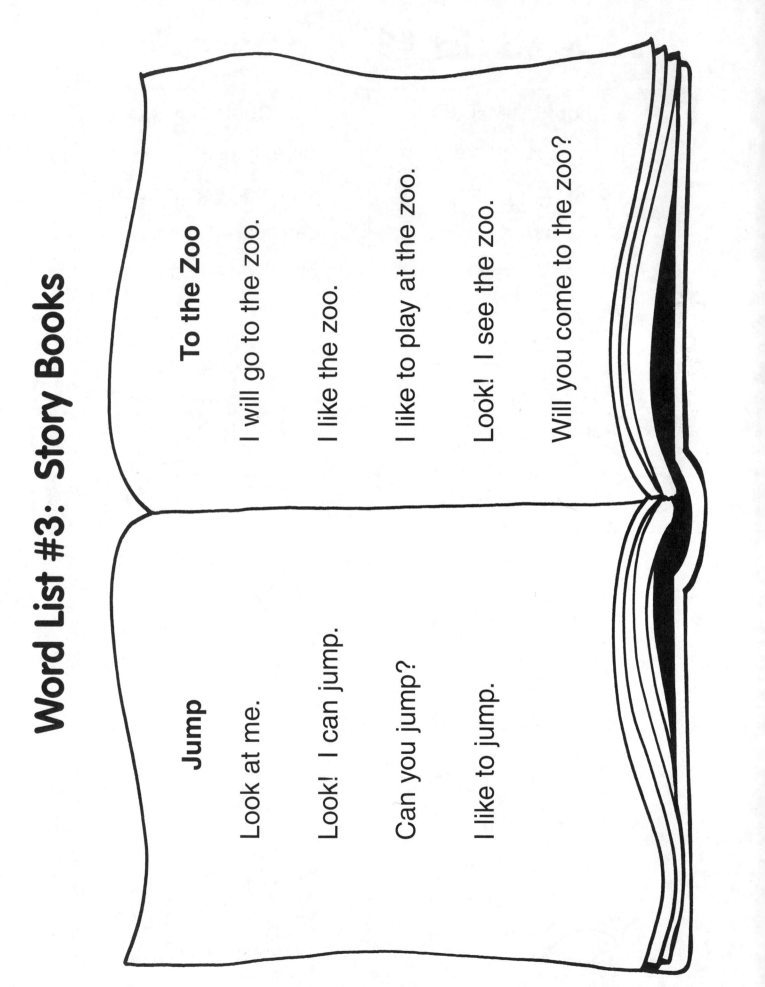

To the Zoo

I will go to the zoo.

I like the zoo.

I like to play at the zoo.

Look! I see the zoo.

Will you come to the zoo?

Jump

Look at me.

Look! I can jump.

Can you jump?

I like to jump.

Word List #3: Story Books

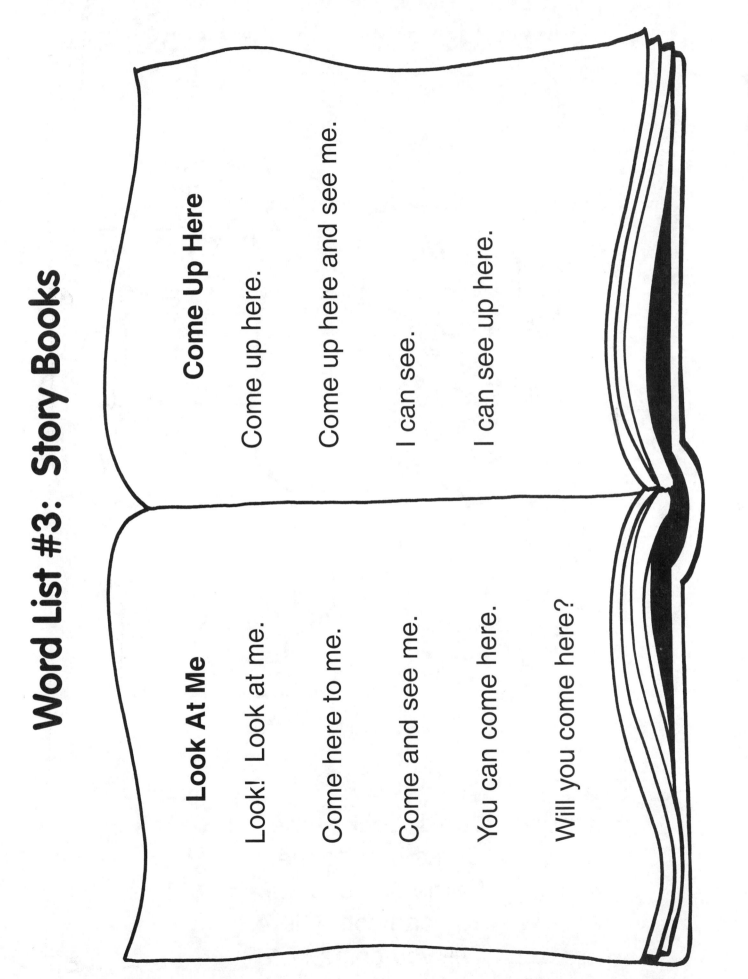

Come Up Here

Come up here.

Come up here and see me.

I can see.

I can see up here.

Look At Me

Look! Look at me.

Come here to me.

Come and see me.

You can come here.

Will you come here?

Word List #3: Library Box

Look At Me

Look! Look at me.
Come here to me.
Come and see me.
You can come here.
Will you come here?

Word List #3: Library Box

Come Up Here

Come up here.
Come up here and see me.
I can see.
I can see up here.

Word List #3: Library Box

Jump

Look at me!
Look! I can jump.
Can you jump?
I like to jump.

Word List #3: Library Box

To the Zoo

I will go to the zoo.
I like the zoo.
I like to play at the zoo.
Look! I see the zoo.
Will you come to the zoo?

Word List #3: Cut-Up Sentences

Come	jump.	to	like	I
me.	see	and	here.	up
here.	up	see	can	I

Word List #3: Cut-Up Sentences

Will you come to the zoo?

I will go to the zoo.

Will you come here?

Word List #3: Running Records

Name: _____   _____ % Accuracy

Date: _____   1: _____ S/C Ratio

"Jump"

(14 Running Words)

	errors	self-corrections
Look at me! Look! I can jump. Can you jump? I like to jump.		
Totals:		

Running Words – Errors = % of Accuracy
Running Words

14 – _____ = _____ % Accuracy

Errors + Self-Corrections (S/C) = S/C Rate
Self-Corrections

_____ + _____ = 1 : _____ S/C Rate

Accuracy Levels
100% – 94% = easy
94% – 90% = instructional
below 90% = frustration

Comments and Observations:

Word List #3: Running Records

Name: _____   _____ % Accuracy

Date: _____   1: _____ S/C Ratio

"To The Zoo"

(28 Running Words)	errors	self-corrections
I will go to the zoo. I like the zoo. I like to play at the zoo. Look! I see the zoo. Will you come to the zoo?		
Totals:		

Running Words – Errors = % of Accuracy
    Running Words

28 – _____ = _____ % Accuracy

Errors + Self-Corrections (S/C) = S/C Rate
    Self-Corrections

_____ + _____ = 1 : ____ S/C Rate

Accuracy Levels
100% – 94% = easy
94% – 90% = instructional
below 90% = frustration

Comments and Observations:

Word List	Times used in stories
1. is	5
2. black	2
3. a	5
4. purple	2
5. he	4
6. with	4
7. big	11
8. do	3

Times Word Is Used in *Each* Story

	"The Big Frog"	"A Purple Cow?"	"Big Black Dog"	"The Big Orange Rat"
1. is	1	0	1	3
2. black	1	0	1	0
3. a	1	2	1	1
4. purple	0	2	0	0
5. he	1	2	0	1
6. with	0	1	3	0
7. big	2	2	2	5
8. do	1	1	1	0

Number of times words from Word Lists #1–#3 are used → 64

Reading Strategies to Review

- Using Known Words
- Checking Pictures For Meaning
- 1:1 Correspondence
- Question Mark

Reading Strategies to Introduce

Suffixes ("ing" and "s")—changing a known word by adding *ing* or *s* to the ending
(look → looking) (like → likes)

Cross-checking initial sounds with meaning (picture)—picture clue is not enough information, student needs to also check first letter sound (for instance, in story #4, picture could be either "rat" or "mouse")

Word List #4: Sight-Word Stories

Story #1 — The Big Frog

I can see a big frog.

Do you see the big frog?

He is black and green.

Look at the frog jump.

(*22 running words*)

Story #2 — A Purple Cow?

Look! I see a big purple cow.

Do you see a big purple cow?

I like the cow and he likes me.

He and I will jump and play.

Come here cow and play with me.

(*17 running words*)

Story #3 — Big Black Dog

Here is a big black dog.

I like to play with the dog.

Do you like to play with the dog?

We can play with the big dog.

(*28 running words*)

Story #4 — The Big Orange Rat

The orange rat is big.

The big orange rat will play.

Look at me, big orange rat.

The big orange rat is looking at me.

He is a big rat.

(*30 running words*)

Word List #4: Flash Cards

is	black
a	purple
he	with
big	do

Word List #4: Homework

The Big Frog

I can see a big frog.

Do you see the big frog?

He is black and green.

Look at the frog jump.

A Purple Cow?

Look! I see a big purple cow.

Do you see a big purple cow?

I like the cow and he likes me.

He and I will jump and play.

Come here cow and play with me.

Big Black Dog

Here is a big black dog.

I like to play with the dog.

Do you like to play with the dog?

We can play with the big dog.

The Big Orange Rat

The orange rat is big.

The big orange rat will play.

Look at me, big orange rat.

The big orange rat is looking at me.

He is a big rat.

Word List #4: Story Books

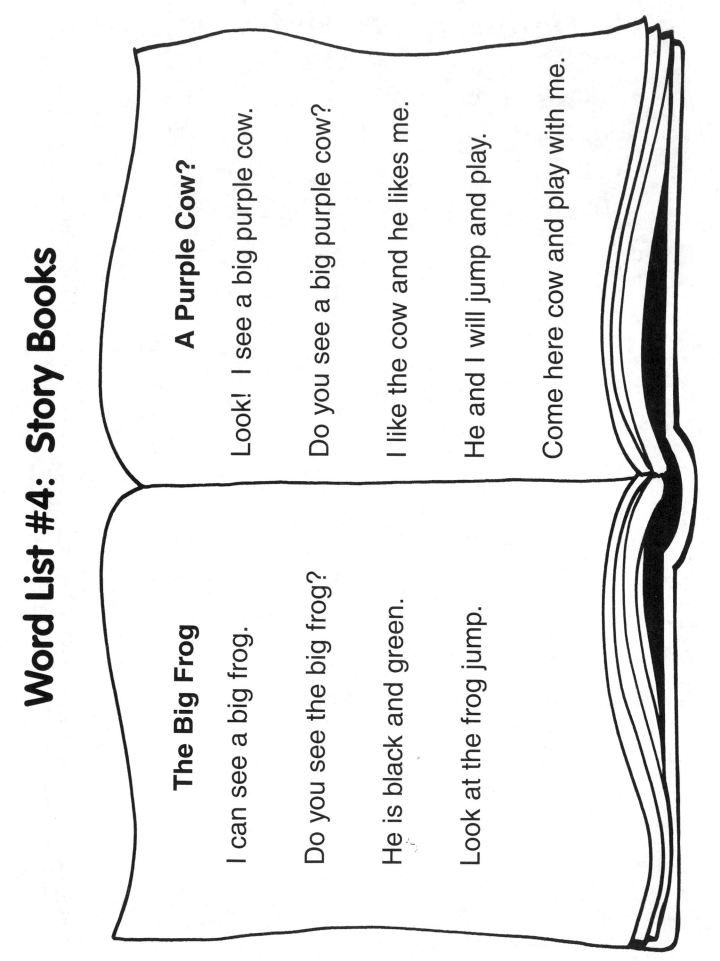

A Purple Cow?

Look! I see a big purple cow.

Do you see a big purple cow?

I like the cow and he likes me.

He and I will jump and play.

Come here cow and play with me.

The Big Frog

I can see a big frog.

Do you see the big frog?

He is black and green.

Look at the frog jump.

Word List #4: Story Books

The Big Orange Rat

The orange rat is big.

The big orange rat will play.

Look at me, big orange rat.

The big orange rat is looking at me.

He is a big rat.

Big Black Dog

Here is a big black dog.

I like to play with the dog.

Do you like to play with the dog?

We can play with the big dog.

Word List #4: Library Box

The Big Frog

I can see a big frog.
Do you see the big frog?
He is black and green.
Look at the frog jump.

Word List #4: Library Box

A Purple Cow?

Look! I see a big purple cow.
Do you see a big purple cow?
I like the cow and he likes me.
He and I will jump and play.
Come here cow and play with me.

Word List #4: Library Box

Big Black Dog

Here is a big black dog.
I like to play with the dog.
Do you like to play with the dog?
We can play with the big dog.

Word List #4: Library Box

The Big Orange Rat

The orange rat is big.
The big orange rat will play.
Look at me, big orange rat.
The big orange rat is looking at me.
He is a big rat.

Word List #4: Cut-Up Sentences

The	big	orange	rat	is	looking
at	me.	Come	here	cow	
and	play	with	me.		

Word List #4: Cut-Up Sentences

He	is	black	and	green.
Here	is	a	big	black	dog.
I	can	see	a	big	frog.

Word List #4: Running Records

Name: _____   _____ % Accuracy

Date: _____   1: _____ S/C Ratio

"The Big Orange Rat"

(*30 Running Words*)

	errors	self-corrections
The orange rat is big. The big orange rat will play. Look at me big orange rat. The big orange rat is looking at me. He is a big rat.		
Totals:		

Running Words – Errors = % of Accuracy
Running Words

30 – _____ = _____ % Accuracy

Errors + Self-Corrections (S/C) = S/C Rate
Self-Corrections

_____ + _____ = 1 : _____ S/C Rate

Accuracy Levels
100% – 94% = easy
94% – 90% = instructional
below 90% = frustration

Comments and Observations:

Word List #4: Running Records

Name: _____   _____ % Accuracy

Date: _____   1: _____ S/C Ratio

"Big Black Dog"

(*28 Running Words*)	errors	self-corrections
Here is a big black dog. I like to play with the dog. Do you like to play with the dog? We can play with the big dog.		
Totals:		

Running Words – Errors = % of Accuracy   28 – _____ = _____ % Accuracy
      Running Words

Errors + Self-Corrections (S/C) = S/C Rate   _____ + _____ = __1 :__ S/C Rate
      Self-Corrections

Accuracy Levels
100% – 94% = easy
94% – 90% = instructional
below 90% = frustration

Comments and Observations:

Word List	Times used in stories
1. help	4
2. said	6
3. on	4
4. it	4
5. my	5
6. little	4
7. boy	6
8. want	6

Times Word Is Used in *Each* Story

	"Bat and Cat"	"Happy Birthday"	"Want to Play?"	"The Spider"
1. help	3	0	0	1
2. said	2	1	2	1
3. on	1	0	0	3
4. it	0	1	0	3
5. my	0	5	0	0
6. little	0	1	2	1
7. boy	0	1	3	2
8. want	0	1	4	1

Number of times words from Word Lists #1–#4 are used → 68

Reading Strategies to Review

- Using Known Words
- Checking Pictures For Meaning
- 1:1 Correspondence
- Question Mark and Exclamation Point
- Suffixes ("s" Ending)

Reading Strategies to Introduce

Blending—decode by sounding through the word (/t/ /o/ /p/ = top)

Quotation Marks (" ")—"talking marks" or someone speaking; recognizing the symbols and the change they cause in intonation and expression when reading.

Comma—recognize symbol and pause when encountered in text ("take a break, but there is more")

Word List #5: Sight-Word Stories

Story #1 — Bat and Cat

The cat jumps up.

He is up on the top.

"Help!" said the cat.

"Here comes the spider."

"I will help you!" said the bat.

"I will help you, cat."

(30 running words)

Story #2 — Happy Birthday

"It is my birthday!" said the little boy.

"Can you come to my party?"

"My party is here."

"I want you to come to my party."

"Will you come to my party?"

(32 running words)

Story #3 — Want to Play?

The little boy wants to play.

"Do you want to play?" said the little boy.

"Do you want to play with me?"

"I want to play with you!" said a big boy.

(32 running words)

Story #4 — The Spider

"Help! I see a spider!" said the little boy.

"Jump on it!"

"Jump on it, big boy!"

"I want you to jump on it!"

(24 running words)

Word List #5: Flash Cards

help	said
on	it
my	little
boy	want

Word List #5: Homework

Bat and Cat

The cat jumps up.

He is up on the top.

"Help!" said the cat.

"Here comes the spider."
-
"I will help you!" said the bat.

"I will help you, cat."

Happy Birthday

"It is my birthday!" said the little boy.

"Can you come to my party?"

"My party is here."

"I want you to come to my party."

"Will you come to my party?"

Want to Play?

The little boy wants to play.

"Do you want to play?" said the little boy.

"Do you want to play with me?"

"I want to play with you!" said a big boy.

The Spider

"Help! I see a spider!" said the little boy.

"Jump on it!"

"Jump on it, big boy!"

"I want you to jump on it!"

Word List #5: Story Books

Happy Birthday

"It is my birthday!" said the little boy.

"Can you come to my party?"

"My party is here."

"I want you to come to my party."

"Will you come to my party?"

Bat and Cat

The cat jumps up.

He is up on the top.

"Help!" said the cat.

"Here comes the spider."

"I will help you!" said the bat.

"I will help you, cat."

Word List #5: Story Books

The Spider

"Help! I see a spider!" said the little boy.

"Jump on it!"

"Jump on it, big boy!"

"I want you to jump on it!"

Want to Play?

The little boy wants to play.

"Do you want to play?" said the little boy.

"Do you want to play with me?"

"I want to play with you!" said a big boy.

Word List #5: Library Box

Bat and Cat

The cat jumps up.
He is up on the top.
"Help!" said the cat.
"Here comes the spider."
"I will help you!" said the bat.
"I will help you, cat."

Word List #5: Library Box

Happy Birthday

"It is my birthday!" said the little boy.
"Can you come to my party?"
"My party is here."
"I want you to come to my party."
"Will you come to my party?"

Word List #5: Library Box

Want to Play?

The little boy wants to play.
"Do you want to play?" said the little boy.
"Do you want to play with me?"
"I want to play with you!" said a big boy.

Word List #5: Library Box

The Spider

"Help! I see a spider!" said the little boy.
"Jump on it!"
"Jump on it, big boy!"
"I want you to jump on it!"

Word List #5: Cut-Up Sentences

He	is	up
on	the	top.

Can	you	come
to	my	party?

The	little	boy
wants	to	play.

Word List #5: Cut-Up Sentences

"Do you want to play with me?"

"I want you to jump on it!"

"Here comes the spider."

Word List #5: Running Records

Name: _____   _____ % Accuracy

Date: _____   1: _____ S/C Ratio

"Want to Play?"

(32 Running Words)   **errors**   **self-corrections**

	errors	self-corrections
The little boy wants to play. "Do you want to play?" said the little boy. "Do you want to play with me?" "I want to play with you!" said the big boy.		
Totals:		

Running Words – Errors = % of Accuracy   32 – _____ = _____ % Accuracy
    Running Words

Errors + Self-Corrections (S/C) = S/C Rate   _____ + _____ = _1 : ____ S/C Rate
    Self-Corrections

Accuracy Levels
100% – 94% = easy
94% – 90% = instructional
below 90% = frustration

Comments and Observations:

Word List #5: Running Records

Name: _____   _____ % Accuracy

Date: _____   1: _____ S/C Ratio

"The Spider"

(24 Running Words)	errors	self-corrections
"Help! I see a spider!" said the little boy. "Jump on it!" "Jump on it big boy!" "I want you to jump on it!"		
Totals:		

Running Words – Errors = % of Accuracy   24 – _____ = _____ % Accuracy
　　　　　Running Words

Errors + Self-Corrections (S/C) = S/C Rate   _____ + _____ = 1 : _____ S/C Rate
　　　　　Self-Corrections

Accuracy Levels
100% – 94% = easy
94% – 90% = instructional
below 90% = frustration

Comments and Observations:

Word List	Times used in stories
1. this	3
2. has	2
3. down	3
4. run	5
5. in	2
6. home	4
7. not	4
8. funny	4

Times Word Is Used in *Each* Story

	"The Boy"	"My Dog"	"Help My Cat!"	"The Funny Cat"
1. this	1	1	1	0
2. has	1	1	0	0
3. down	0	0	3	0
4. run	1	1	0	3
5. in	0	0	2	0
6. home	0	1	0	3
7. not	0	1	2	1
8. funny	0	0	2	2

Number of times words from Word Lists #1–#5 are used → 68

Reading Strategies to Review

- Using Known Words
- Checking Pictures For Meaning
- 1:1 Correspondence
- Question Mark and Exclamation Point
- Suffixes ("s" Ending)
- Blending (/s/ /p/ /o/ /t/ /s/ = spots)
- Quotation Marks (" ")
- Comma

Reading Strategies to Introduce

Chunking—using the rime portion of a word to create new words by replacing the initial sound ("at" chunk = cat/rat/hat)

Word List #6: Sight-Word Stories

Story #1 — The Boy

This is a boy.

He has a little ball.

He wants to play.

Do you want to play?

He will run and play.

(23 running words)

Story #2 — My Dog

This is my dog.

My dog is not red.

He has black spots.

He likes to jump on me.

We like to run home.

(24 running words)

Story #3 — Help My Cat!

"Help!" said the boy in the funny hat.

"My yellow cat is in the tree."

"He can not come down!"

"Come down, cat!"

"This is not funny, cat!"

"Come down to me, cat!"

(33 running words)

Story #4 — The Funny Cat

Run, funny cat, run!

Do not come here, funny cat.

Run home to the little boy.

The boy is at home.

Go home to the little boy.

(27 running words)

Word List #6: Flash Cards

this	has
down	run
in	home
not	funny

Word List #6: Homework

The Boy

This is a boy.

He has a little ball.

He wants to play.

Do you want to play?
-
He will run and play.

My Dog

This is my dog.

My dog is not red.

He has black spots.

He likes to jump on me.

We like to run home.

Help My Cat!

"Help!" said the boy in the funny hat.

"My yellow cat is in the tree."

"He can not come down!"

"Come down, cat!"

"This is not funny, cat!"

"Come down to me, cat!"

The Funny Cat

Run, funny cat, run!

Do not come here, funny cat.

Run home to the little boy.

The boy is at home.

Go home to the little boy.

Word List #6: Story Books

My Dog

This is my dog.

My dog is not red.

He has black spots.

He likes to jump on me.

We like to run home.

The Boy

This is a boy.

He has a little ball.

He wants to play.

Do you want to play?

He will run and play.

Word List #6: Story Books

The Funny Cat

Run, funny cat, run!

Do not come here, funny cat.

Run home to the little boy.

The boy is at home.

Go home to the little boy.

Help My Cat

"Help!" said the boy in the funny hat.

"My yellow cat is in the tree."

"He can not come down!"

"Come down, cat!"

"This is not funny, cat!"

"Come down to me, cat!"

Word List #6: Library Box

The Boy

This is a boy.
He has a little ball.
He wants to play.
Do you want to play?
He will run and play.

Word List #6: Library Box

My Dog

This is my dog.
My dog is not red.
He has black spots.
He likes to jump on me.
We like to run home.

Word List #6: Library Box

Help My Cat!
"Help!" said the boy in the funny hat.
"My yellow cat is in the tree."
"He can not come down!"
"Come down, cat!"
"This is not funny, cat!'
"Come down to me, cat!"

Word List #6: Library Box

The Funny Cat

Run, funny cat, run.
Do not come here, funny cat.
Run home to the little boy.
The boy is at home.
Go home to the little boy.

Word List #6: Cut-Up Sentences

black	has	He	dog.	my	is	This

little	the	to	home	Run	spots.

home.	at	is	boy	The.	boy.

Word List #6: Cut-Up Sentences

"My yellow cat is in the tree!"

"This is not funny, cat!"

He has a little ball.

Word List #6: Running Records

Name: _____   _____ % Accuracy

Date: _____   1: _____ S/C Ratio

"Help My Cat"

(33 Running Words)	errors	self-corrections
"Help!" said the boy in the funny hat. "My yellow cat is in the tree." "He can not come down!" "Come down, cat!" "This is not funny, cat!" "Come down to me, cat!"		
Totals:		

Running Words – Errors = % of Accuracy
    Running Words

33 – _____ = _____ % Accuracy

Errors + Self-Corrections (S/C) = S/C Rate
    Self-Corrections

_____ + _____ = 1 : ___ S/C Rate

Accuracy Levels
100% – 94% = easy
94% – 90% = instructional
below 90% = frustration

Comments and Observations:

Word List #6: Running Records

Name: _____   _____ % Accuracy

Date: _____   1: _____ S/C Ratio

"The Funny Cat"

(*27 Running Words*)

	errors	self-corrections
Run, funny cat, run! Do not come here, funny cat. Run home to the little boy. The boy is at home. Go home to the little boy.		
Totals:		

Running Words – Errors = % of Accuracy   27 – _____ = _____ % Accuracy
Running Words

Errors + Self-Corrections (S/C) = S/C Rate   _____ + _____ = 1 : ___ S/C Rate
Self-Corrections

Accuracy Levels
100% – 94% = easy
94% – 90% = instructional
below 90% = frustration

Comments and Observations:

Word List	Times used in stories
1. she	3
2. for	4
3. get	4
4. please	2
5. have	3
6. some	5
7. am	4
8. after	2

Times Word Is Used in *Each* Story

	"Funny Little Frog"	"Come Home"	"The Dog and the Moon"	"Flowers for Mom"
1. she	0	2	0	1
2. for	0	1	1	2
3. get	0	1	0	3
4. please	0	1	0	1
5. have	1	1	0	1
6. some	1	0	0	4
7. am	2	1	1	0
8. after	0	1	1	0

Number of times words from Word List #1–#6 are used → 15

Reading Strategies to Review

- Using Known Words
- Checking Pictures For Meaning
- 1:1 Correspondence
- Question Mark and Exclamation Point
- Suffixes ("s" Ending)
- Blending (/s/ /p/ /o/ /t/ /s/ = spots)
- Quotation Marks (" ")
- Comma

Reading Strategies to Introduce

Using Known Words—using a familiar word to decode an unfamiliar word (example: "see" to "seed"; "at" to "that")

Wrap-Around Sentence—sentence does not end at the end of the line, but "wraps-around" to the next line

Word List #7: Sight-Word Stories

Story #1 – Funny Little Frog

I am a funny little frog.

I am green and I have some yellow spots.

I can jump up and down!

Can you?

(*23 running words*)

Story #2 – Come Home

Will you help me, please?

I am looking for my cat.

She has run after a mouse.

I have to get my cat.

She has to come home with me.

(*30 running words*)

Story #3 — The Dog and the Moon

I am a dog.

After the moon comes up,

I like to jump at the moon.

I like to run for the moon.

(*23 running words*)

Story #4 — Flowers for Mom

I have to get some flowers for my mom.

She is at home and wants some flowers.

Please, will you help me get some flowers for my mom?

I will help you get some flowers.

(*35 running words*)

Word List #7: Flash Cards

she	for
get	please
have	some
am	after

Word List #7: Homework

Funny Little Frog

I am a funny little frog.

I am green, and I have some yellow spots.

I can jump up and down!

Can you?

Come Home

Will you help me, please?

I am looking for my cat.

She has run after a mouse.

I have to get my cat.

She has to come home with me.

The Dog and the Moon

I am a dog.

After the moon comes up,

I like to jump at the moon.

I like to run for the moon.

Flowers for Mom

I have to get some flowers for my mom.

She is at home and wants some flowers.

Please will you help me get some flowers for my mom?

I will help you get some flowers.

Word List #7: Story Books

Come Home

Will you help me please?

I am looking for my cat.

She has run after a mouse.

I have to get my cat.

She has to come home with me.

Funny Little Frog

I am a funny little frog.

I am green, and I have some yellow spots.

I can jump up and down!

Can you?

Word List #7: Story Books

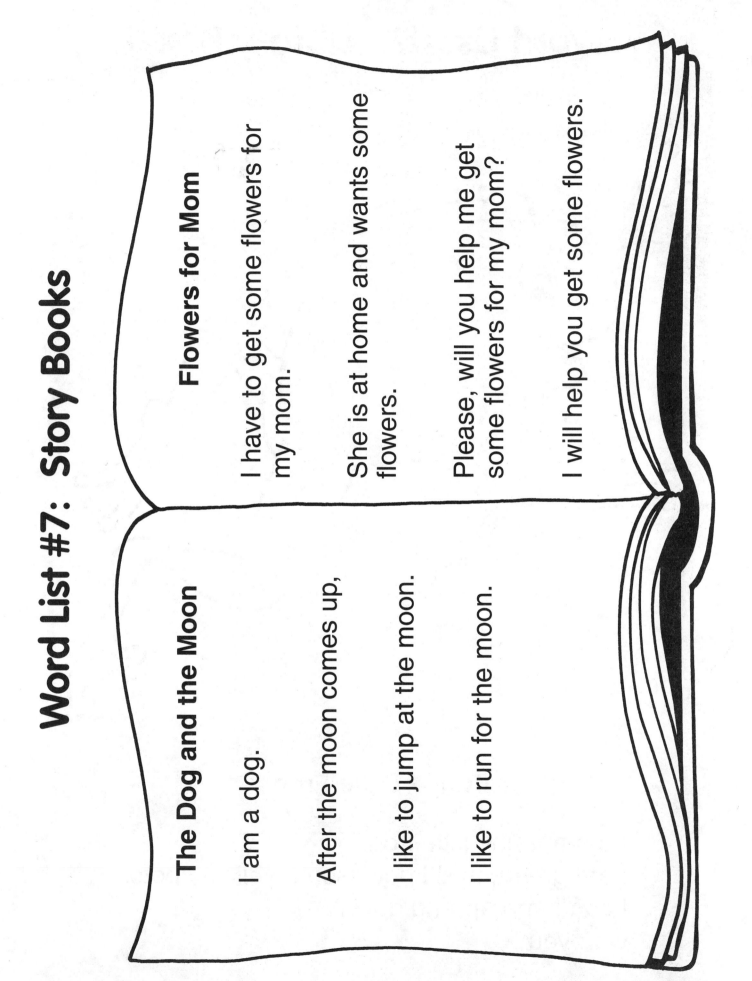

Flowers for Mom

I have to get some flowers for my mom.

She is at home and wants some flowers.

Please, will you help me get some flowers for my mom?

I will help you get some flowers.

The Dog and the Moon

I am a dog.

After the moon comes up,

I like to jump at the moon.

I like to run for the moon.

#3225 Reproducible Little Books

Word List #7: Library Box

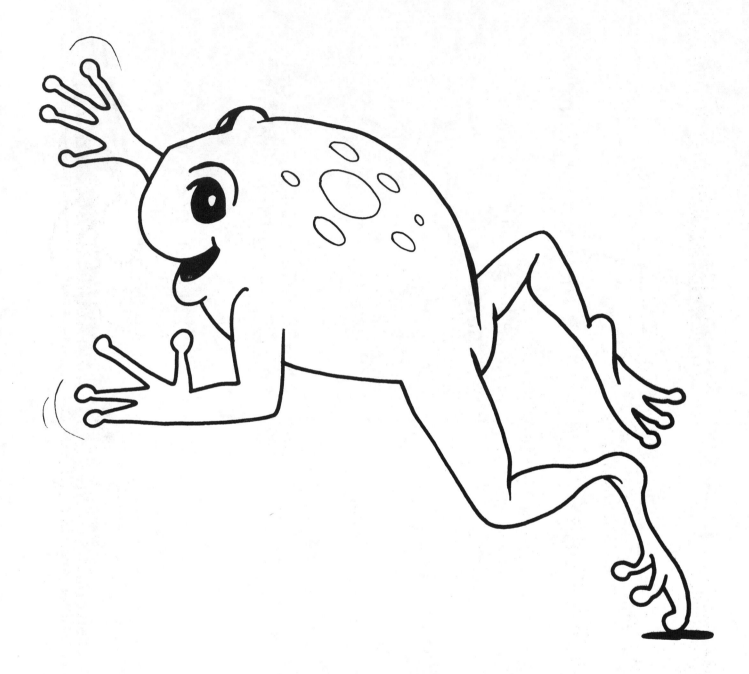

Funny Little Frog

I am a funny little frog.
I am green, and I have some yellow spots.
I can jump up and down!
Can you?

Word List #7: Library Box

Come Home

Will you help me, please?
I am looking for my cat.
She has run after a mouse.
I have to get my cat.
She has to come home with me.

Word List #7: Library Box

The Dog and the Moon

I am a dog.
After the moon comes up,
I like to jump at the moon.
I like to run for the moon.

Word List #7: Library Box

Flowers for Mom

I have to get some flowers for my mom.
She is at home and wants some flowers.
Please, will you help me get some flowers
for my mom?
I will help you get some flowers.

Word List #7: Cut-Up Sentences

flowers		
some	at home	
get	She	flowers.
to	is	
have	my mom.	some.
I	for	wants
		and

Word List #7: Cut-Up Sentences

I	am	a	funny	little	frog.

She	has	run	after	a	mouse.

I	am	looking	for	my	cat.

Word List #7: Running Records

Name: _____   _____ % Accuracy

Date: _____   1: _____ S/C Ratio

"The Dog and the Moon"

(23 Running Words)

	errors	self-corrections
I am a dog. After the moon comes up, I like to jump at the moon. I like to run for the moon.		
Totals:		

Running Words – Errors = % of Accuracy   23 – _____ = _____ % Accuracy
Running Words

Errors + Self-Corrections (S/C) = S/C Rate   _____ + _____ = 1 : ___ S/C Rate
Self-Corrections

Accuracy Levels
100% – 94% = easy
94% – 90% = instructional
below 90% = frustration

Comments and Observations:

Word List #7: Running Records

Name: _____   _____ % Accuracy

Date: _____   1: _____ S/C Ratio

"Flowers For Mom"

(35 Running Words)	errors	self-corrections
I have to get some flowers for my mom. She is at home and wants some flowers Please, will you help me get some flowers for my mom? I will help you get some flowers.		
Totals:		

Running Words – Errors = % of Accuracy
   Running Words

<u> 35 </u> – _____ = _____ % Accuracy

Errors + Self-Corrections (S/C) = S/C Rate
   Self-Corrections

_____ + _____ = <u> 1 : </u>_____ S/C Rate

Accuracy Levels
100% – 94% = easy
94% – 90% = instructional
below 90% = frustration

Comments and Observations:

Word List	Times used in stories
1. yes	2
2. ran	4
3. but	3
4. by	2
5. saw	6
6. away	6
7. eat	5
8. when	3

Times Word Is Used in *Each* Story

	"Watermelon"	"I Saw A Little Dog"	"An Egg for Bunny"	"The Lamb"
1. yes	1	0	0	1
2. ran	0	1	1	2
3. but	1	1	0	1
4. by	0	1	1	0
5. saw	0	2	2	2
6. away	0	2	1	3
7. eat	2	0	0	3
8. when	1	1	1	0

Number of times words from Word Lists #1–#7 are used → 65

Reading Strategies to Review

- Using Known Words to Decode Unknown Words
- Checking Pictures For Meaning
- 1:1 Correspondence
- Question Mark and Exclamation Point
- Suffixes ("s" Ending)
- Blending (/s/ /p/ /o/ /t/ /s/ = spots)
- Quotation Marks (" ")
- Cross-checking initial sounds with meaning (picture)
- Comma
- Wrap-Around Sentences

Reading Strategies to Introduce

Using Known Words—using a familiar word to decode an unfamiliar word (example: "see" to "seed"; "at" to "that")

Word List #8: Sight-Word Stories

Story #1 — Watermelon

Yes! I do like watermelon.

I like to eat watermelon.

Watermelon is red, but it has black seeds.

I look funny when I eat watermelon.

(*25 running words*)

Story #2 — I Saw A Little Dog

I saw a little dog by the apples.

But he ran away when he saw me.

Come here little dog.

Do not run away.

(*24 running words*)

Story #3 — An Egg for Bunny

The little bunny saw eggs by the basket.

"When will I get an egg?" he said.

He saw the egg that he wanted and he ran away with it.

(*29 running words*)

Story #4 — The Lamb

Yes! I saw the lamb.

I saw it eat some flowers, but it ran away.

It ran away home.

Run away lamb. Do not eat the flowers.

We do not want you to eat the flowers.

(*36 running words*)

Word List #8: Flash Cards

yes	ran
but	by
saw	away
eat	when

Word List #8: Homework

Watermelon

Yes! I do like watermelon.

I like to eat watermelon.

Watermelon is red, but it has black seeds.

I look funny when I eat watermelon.

I Saw A Little Dog

I saw a little dog by the apples.

But he ran away when he saw me.

Come here little dog.

Do not run away.

An Egg for Bunny

The little bunny saw eggs by the basket.

"When will I get an egg?" he said.

He saw the egg that he wanted and he ran away with it.

The Lamb

Yes, I saw the lamb.

I saw it eat some flowers, but it ran away.

It ran away home.

Run away lamb. Do not eat the flowers.

We do not want you to eat the flowers.

Word List #8: Story Books

I Saw A Little Dog

I saw a little dog by the apples.

But he ran away when he saw me.

Come here little dog.

Do not run away.

Watermelon

Yes! I do like watermelon.

I like to eat watermelon.

Watermelon is red, but it has black seeds.

I look funny when I eat watermelon.

Word List #8: Story Books

The Lamb

Yes, I saw the lamb.

I saw it eat some flowers, but it ran away.

It ran away home.

Run away lamb. Do not eat the flowers.

We do not want you to eat the flowers.

An Egg for Bunny

The little bunny saw eggs by the basket.

"When will I get an egg?" he said.

He saw the egg that he wanted and he ran away with it.

Word List #8: Library Box

Watermelon

Yes! I do like watermelon.
I like to eat watermelon.
Watermelon is red, but it has black seeds.
I look funny when I eat watermelon.

Word List #8: Library Box

I Saw A Little Dog

I saw a little dog by the apples.
But he ran away when he saw me.
Come here little dog.
Do not run away.

Word List #8: Library Box

An Egg for Bunny

The little bunny saw eggs by the basket.
"When will I get an egg?" he said.
He saw the egg that he wanted and he ran away with it.

Word List #8: Library Box

The Lamb

Yes, I saw the lamb.
I saw it eat some flowers, but it ran away.
It ran away home.
Run away lamb. Do not eat the flowers.
We do not want you to eat the flowers.

Word List #8: Cut-Up Sentences

the	saw	do
by	bunny	We
dog	little	the basket.
little	The	by
a	apples.	the eggs
saw		the
I		

Word List #8: Cut-Up Sentences

not want you to eat the flowers.

Watermelon is red, but it has

black seeds. I saw the lamb.

Word List #8: Running Records

Name: _____   _____ % Accuracy

Date: _____   1: _____ S/C Ratio

"An Egg For Bunny"

(29 Running Words)	errors	self-corrections
The little bunny saw eggs by the basket. "When will I get an egg?" he said. He saw the egg that he wanted and he ran away with it.		
Totals:		

Running Words – Errors = % of Accuracy
Running Words   29 – _____ = _____ % Accuracy

Errors + Self-Corrections (S/C) = S/C Rate
Self-Corrections   _____ + _____ = 1 : _____ S/C Rate

Accuracy Levels
100% – 94% = easy
94% – 90% = instructional
below 90% = frustration

Comments and Observations:

Word List #8: Running Records

Name: _____ _____ % Accuracy

Date: _____ 1: _____ S/C Ratio

"The Lamb"

(*36 Running Words*)	errors	self-corrections
Yes! I saw the lamb. I saw it eat some flowers, but it ran away. It ran away home. Run away lamb. Do not eat the flowers. We do not want you to eat the flowers.		
Totals:		

Running Words – Errors = % of Accuracy   36 – _____ = _____ % Accuracy
    Running Words

Errors + Self-Corrections (S/C) = S/C Rate   _____ + _____ = 1 : _____ S/C Rate
    Self-Corrections

Accuracy Levels
100% – 94% = easy
94% – 90% = instructional
below 90% = frustration

Comments and Observations:

Word List	Times used in stories
1. are	7
2. good	2
3. went	4
4. they	3
5. where	4
6. all	4
7. one	5
8. friend	5

Times Word Is Used in *Each* Story

	"The Girl and the Flowers"	"My Friend"	"Balloons!"	"At the Beach"
1. are	3	1	2	1
2. good	0	2	0	0
3. went	1	0	1	2
4. they	1	0	2	0
5. where	3	0	0	1
6. all	2	0	2	0
7. one	0	0	5	0
8. friend	0	4	0	1

Number of times words from Word Lists #1–#8 are used → 71

Reading Strategies to Review

- Using Known Words
- Checking Pictures For Meaning
- 1:1 Correspondence
- Question Mark and Exclamation Point
- Suffixes ("s" Ending)
- Quotation Marks (" ")
- Cross-checking initial sounds with meaning (picture)
- Comma
- Wrap-Around Sentences

Word List #9: Sight-Word Stories

Story #1 —
The Girl and the Flowers

The girl went to look for some flowers.

"Where are all the flowers?" said the girl.

"I want some flowers."

"Where are they?"

"Where are all the flowers?"

(*28 running words*)

Story #2 — My Friend

This is my friend.

We are good friends.

My friend and I like to play.

She is my good friend!

(*20 running words*)

Story #3 — Balloons!

Look! I went to get some balloons.

They are all hearts.

One is blue.

One is red.

One is green.

One is orange.

And one is purple.

They are all for me!

(*32 running words*)

Story #4 — At the Beach

Here we are!

My friend and I went to the beach.

We went to the beach for some fun.

Where do you like to go to have fun?

Do you like to go to the beach?

(*36 running words*)

Word List #9: Flash Cards

are	good
went	they
where	all
one	friend

Word List #9: Homework

The Girl and the Flowers

The girl went to look for some flowers.

"Where are all the flowers?" said the girl.

"I want some flowers."

"Where are they?"

"Where are all the flowers?"

My Friend

This is my friend.

We are good friends.

My friend and I like to play.

She is my good friend!

Balloons!

Look! I went to get some balloons.

They are all hearts.

One is blue.

One is red.

One is green.

One is orange.

And one is purple.

They are all for me!

At the Beach

Here we are!

My friend and I went to the beach.

We went to the beach for some fun.

Where do you like to go to have fun?

Do you like to go to the beach?

Word List #9: Story Books

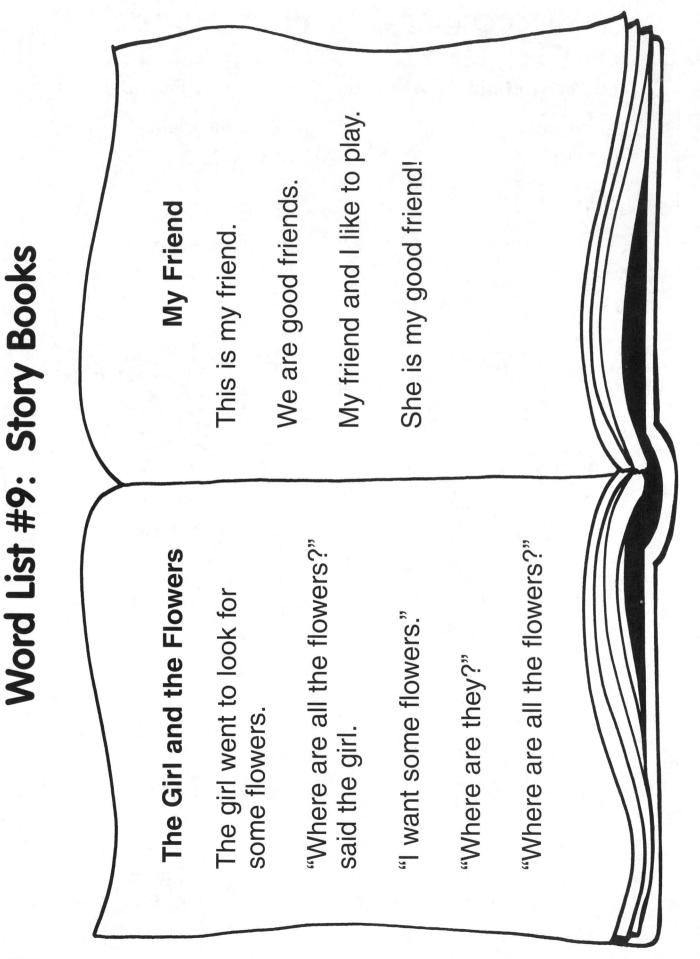

My Friend

This is my friend.

We are good friends.

My friend and I like to play.

She is my good friend!

The Girl and the Flowers

The girl went to look for some flowers.

"Where are all the flowers?" said the girl.

"I want some flowers."

"Where are they?"

"Where are all the flowers?"

Word List #9: Story Books

At the Beach

Here we are!

My friend and I went to the beach.

We went to the beach for some fun.

Where do you like to have fun?

Do you like to go to go to the beach?

Balloons!

Look! I went to get some balloons.

They are all hearts.

One is blue.

One is red.

One is green.

One is orange.

And one is purple.

They are all for me!

Word List #9: Library Box

The Girl and the Flowers

The girl went to look for some flowers.
"Where are all the flowers?" said the girl.
"I want some flowers."
"Where are they?"
"Where are all the flowers?"

Word List #9: Library Box

My Friend

This is my friend.
We are good friends.
My friend and I like to play.
She is my good friend!

#3225 Reproducible Little Books

Word List #9: Library Box

Balloons!

Look! I went to get some balloons.
They are all hearts.
One is blue.
One is red.
One is green.
One is orange.
And one is purple.
They are all for me!

Word List #9: Library Box

At the Beach

Here we are!
My friend and I went to the beach.
We went to the beach for some fun.
Where do you like to go to have fun?
Do you like to go to the beach?

Word List #9: Cut-Up Sentences

My	friend	and	I	went	to	the

beach.	"Where	are	all	the	flowers?"

said	the	girl.	One	is	orange.

Word List #9: Cut-Up Sentences

I	went	to	get	some	balloons.

She	is	my	good	friend!	Where

do	you	like	to	go	to	have	fun?

Word List #9: Running Records

Name: _____   _____ % Accuracy

Date: _____   1: _____ S/C Ratio

"Balloons!"

(*32 Running Words*)	errors	self-corrections
Look! I went to get some balloons. They are all hearts. One is blue. One is red. One is green. One is orange. And one is purple. They are all for me!		
Totals:		

Running Words – Errors = % of Accuracy   32 – _____ = _____ % Accuracy
  Running Words

Errors + Self-Corrections (S/C) = S/C Rate   _____ + _____ = _1 :___ S/C Rate
  Self-Corrections

Accuracy Levels
100% – 94% = easy
94% – 90% = instructional
below 90% = frustration

Comments and Observations:

Word List #9: Running Records

Name: _____   _____ % Accuracy

Date: _____   1: _____ S/C Ratio

"At the Beach"

(*36 Running Words*)	errors	self-corrections
Here we are! My friend and I went to the beach. We went to the beach for some fun. Where do you like to go to have fun? Do you like to go to the beach?		
Totals:		

<u>Running Words – Errors</u> = % of Accuracy   <u>36 – _____</u> = _____ % Accuracy
   Running Words

<u>Errors + Self-Corrections (S/C)</u> = S/C Rate   _____ + _____ = <u>1 :</u> ____ S/C Rate
   Self-Corrections

Accuracy Levels
100% – 94% = easy
94% – 90% = instructional
below 90% = frustration

Comments and Observations:

Word List	Times used in stories
1. what	3
2. make	6
3. so	3
4. tell	2
5. use	3
6. out	5
7. put	4
8. today	4

Times Word Is Used in *Each* Story

	"Want To Eat?"	"My Umbrella"	"It Is Hot!"	"Snowman"
1. what	2	0	0	1
2. make	3	0	0	3
3. so	1	0	2	0
4. tell	1	0	0	1
5. use	0	1	1	1
6. out	0	1	2	2
7. put	0	1	2	1
8. today	0	0	2	2

Number of times words from Word Lists #1–#9 are used → 97

Reading Strategies to Review

- Using Known Words
- Checking Pictures For Meaning
- Question Mark and Exclamation Point
- Suffixes ("s" Ending)
- Quotation Marks (" ")
- Cross-Checking Initial Sounds with Meaning
- Comma
- Blending
- Chunking
- Wrap-Around Sentences

Word List #10: Sight-Word Stories

Story #1 — Want to Eat?

What do you like to eat?

I can make it for you.

I will make it and you can eat it.

So tell me, what do you want me to make for you?

(33 running words)

Story #2 — My Umbrella

This is my umbrella.

I use it when I go out in the rain.

You put it up in the rain.

It is good to have an umbrella when it rains.

(31 running words)

Story #3 — It Is Hot!

It is so hot today!

Get the hose out and put some water on me.

Get the hose out and use it to put some water on me.

It is so hot today!

(33 running words)

Story #4 — Snowman

What can we do today?

We can go out and make a snowman.

We can use a carrot for the nose and put a big hat on it.

Yes! We can go out and make a snowman.

Tell me, do you want to make a snowman today?

(47 running words)

Word List #10: Flash Cards

what	make
so	tell
use	out
put	today

Word List #10: Homework

Want to Eat?

What do you like to eat?

I can make if for you.

I will make it and you can eat it.

So tell me, what do you want me to make for you?

My Umbrella

This is my umbrella.

I use it when I go out in the rain.

You put it up in the rain.

It is good to have an umbrella when it rains.

It Is Hot!

It is so hot today!

Get the hose out and put some water on me.

Get the hose out and use it to put some water on me.

It is so hot today!

Snowman

What can we do today?

We can go out and make a snowman.

We can use a carrot for the nose and put a big hat on it.

Yes! We can go out and make a snowman.

Tell me, do you want to make a snowman today?

Word List #10: Story Books

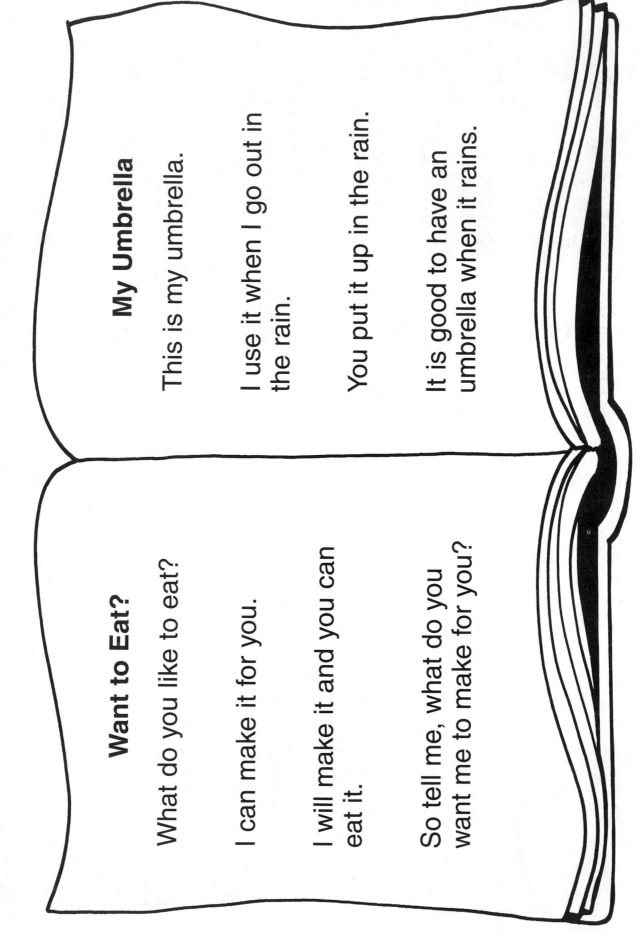

My Umbrella

This is my umbrella.

I use it when I go out in the rain.

You put it up in the rain.

It is good to have an umbrella when it rains.

Want to Eat?

What do you like to eat?

I can make it for you.

I will make it and you can eat it.

So tell me, what do you want me to make for you?

Word List #10: Story Books

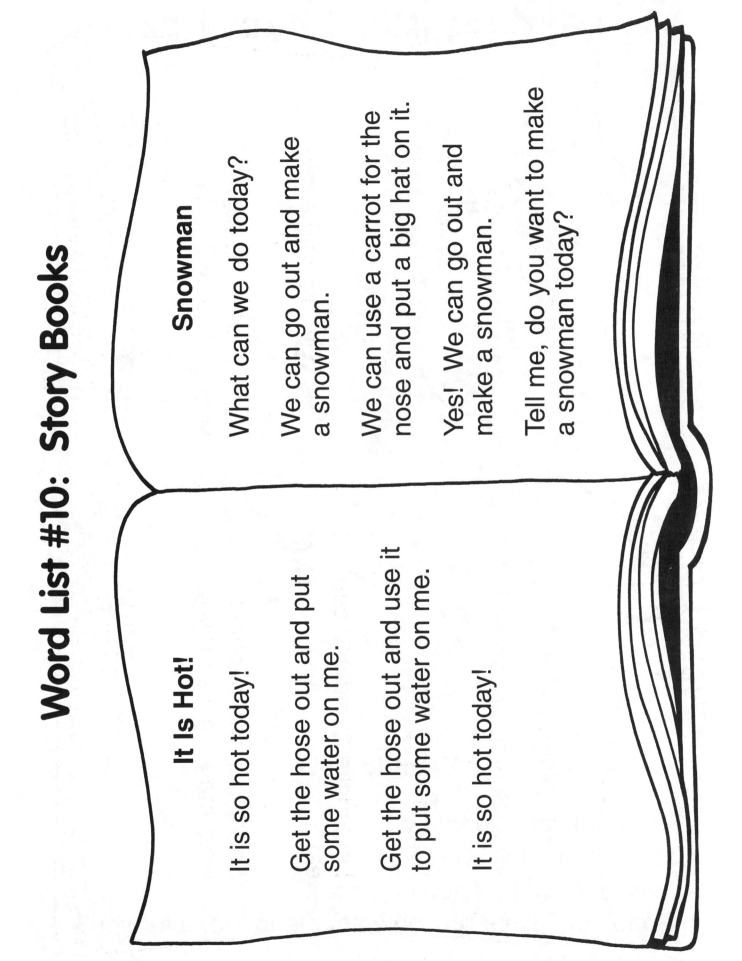

Snowman

What can we do today?

We can go out and make a snowman.

We can use a carrot for the nose and put a big hat on it.

Yes! We can go out and make a snowman.

Tell me, do you want to make a snowman today?

It Is Hot!

It is so hot today!

Get the hose out and put some water on me.

Get the hose out and use it to put some water on me.

It is so hot today!

Word List #10: Library Box

Want to Eat?

What do you like to eat?
I can make it for you.
I will make it and you can eat it.
So tell me, what do you want me to make for you?

Word List #10: Library Box

My Umbrella

This is my umbrella.
I use it when I go out in the rain.
You put it up in the rain.
It is good to have an umbrella when it rains.

Word List #10: Library Box

It Is Hot!

It is so hot today!
Get the hose out and put some water on me.
Get the hose out and use it to put some water on me.
It is so hot today!

Word List #10: Library Box

Snowman

What can we do today?
We can go out and make a snowman.
We can use a carrot for the nose and put a big hat on it.
Yes! We can go out and make a snowman.
Tell me, do you want to make a snowman today?

Word List #10: Cut-Up Sentences

I use it to go out in the rain.

We can go out and make a

This is my umbrella.

snowman.

Word List #10: Cut-Up Sentences

What	do	you	like	to	eat?

What	can	we	do	today?

| You | put | it | up | in | the | rain. |

Word List #10: Running Records

Name: _____   _____ % Accuracy

Date: _____   1: _____ S/C Ratio

"It Is Hot"

(*33 Running Words*)

	errors	self-corrections
It is so hot today! Get the hose out and put some water on me. Get the hose out and use it to put some water on me. It is so hot today!		
Totals:		

Running Words − Errors = % of Accuracy
Running Words

33 − _____ = _____ % Accuracy

Errors + Self-Corrections (S/C) = S/C Rate
Self-Corrections

_____ + _____ = 1 : _____ S/C Rate

Accuracy Levels
100% − 94% = easy
94% − 90% = instructional
below 90% = frustration

Comments and Observations:

Word List #10: Running Records

Name: _____   _____ % Accuracy

Date: _____   1: _____ S/C Ratio

"Snowman"

(*47 Running Words*)	errors	self-corrections
What can we do today? We can go out and make a snowman. We can use a carrot for the nose and put a big hat on it. Yes! We can go out and make a snowman. Tell me, do you want to make a snowman today?		
Totals:		

Running Words − Errors = % of Accuracy   47 − _____ = _____ % Accuracy
    Running Words

Errors + Self-Corrections (S/C) = S/C Rate   _____ + _____ = 1 : ___ S/C Rate
    Self-Corrections

Accuracy Levels
100% − 94% = easy
94% − 90% = instructional
below 90% = frustration

Comments and Observations:

Word List	Times used in stories
1. ride	4
2. new	4
3. take	6
4. fast	5
5. was	5
6. very	3
7. got	3
8. did	3

Times Word Is Used in *Each* Story

	"My New Car"	"Soccer"	"My Big Fish"	"I Went to the Zoo"
1. ride	2	0	0	2
2. new	3	1	0	0
3. take	1	1	1	3
4. fast	1	2	1	1
5. was	0	3	1	1
6. very	0	2	0	1
7. got	0	0	1	2
8. did	0	2	1	0

Number of times words from Word Lists #1–#10 are used → 88

Reading Strategies to Review

- Using Known Words
- Checking Pictures For Meaning
- Question Mark and Exclamation Point
- Quotation Marks (" ")
- Cross-Checking Initial Sounds with Meaning
- Comma
- Blending
- Wrap-Around Sentences

Word List #11: Sight-Word Stories

Story #1 — My New Car

This is my new car.

We can take my new car for a fast ride.

Do you want to go for a ride with me in my new car?

Where do you want to go?

(*35 running words*)

Story #2 — Soccer

Did you play soccer today? I did.

It was fun to take a new ball out and run fast.

I can run very fast.

It was very hot, but it was fun.

(*32 running words*)

Story #3 — My Big Fish

I got a fish!

It was big and fast.

Did you see my big fish?

I will take it home and eat it.

(*23 running words*)

Story #4 — I Went to the Zoo

I got to go to the zoo today.

I got to take a ride on a giraffe.

He was very big and fast.

I said, "Take me for a ride, giraffe!"

He said, "Where do you want me to take you?"

(*41 running words*)

Word List #11: Flash Cards

ride	new
take	fast
was	very
got	did

Word List #11: Homework

My New Car

This is my new car.

We can take my new car for a fast ride.

Do you want to go for a ride with me in my new car?

Where do you want to go?

Soccer

Did you play soccer today?
I did!

It was fun to take a new ball out and run fast.

I can run very fast.

It was very hot, but it was fun.

My Big Fish

I got a fish!

It was big and fast.

Did you see my big fish?

I will take it home and eat it.

I Went to the Zoo

I got to go to the zoo today.

I got to take a ride on a giraffe.

He was very big and fast.

I said, "Take me for a ride, giraffe!"

He said, "Where do you want me to take you?"

Word List #11: Story Books

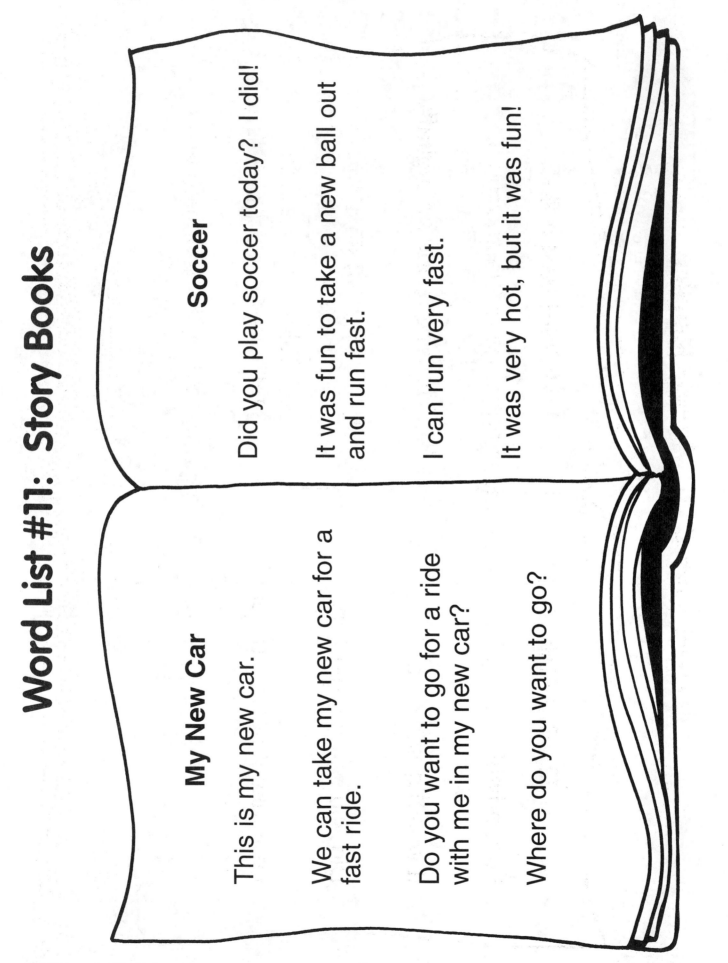

Soccer

Did you play soccer today? I did!

It was fun to take a new ball out and run fast.

I can run very fast.

It was very hot, but it was fun!

My New Car

This is my new car.

We can take my new car for a fast ride.

Do you want to go for a ride with me in my new car?

Where do you want to go?

Word List #11: Story Books

I Went to the Zoo

I got to go to the zoo today.

I got to take a ride on a giraffe.

He was very big and fast.

I said, "Take me for a ride, giraffe!"

He said, "Where do you want me to take you?"

My Big Fish

I got a fish!

It was big and fast.

Did you see my big fish?

I will take it home and eat it!

Word List #11: Library Box

My New Car

This is my new car.
We can take my new car for a fast ride.
Do you want to go for a ride with me in my new car?
Where do you want to go?

Word List #11: Library Box

Soccer

Did you play soccer today? I did!
It was fun to take a new ball out and run fast.
I can run very fast.
It was very hot, but it was fun!

Word List #11: Library Box

My Big Fish

I got a fish!
It was big and fast.
Did you see my big fish?
I will take it home and eat it.

Word List #11: Library Box

I Went to the Zoo

I got to go to the zoo today.
I got to take a ride on a giraffe.
He was very big and fast.
I said, "Take me for a ride, giraffe!"
He said, "Where do you want me to take you?"

Word List #11: Cut-Up Sentences

"Take	me	for	a	ride, giraffe!"
It	was	very	hot,	but it was fun.
Did	you	see	my	big fish?

Word List #11: Cut-Up Sentences

We	can	take	my	new	car	for

a	fast	ride.	I	will	take	it

home	and	eat	it.

Word List #11: Running Records

Name: _____   _____ % Accuracy

Date: _____   1: _____ S/C Ratio

"My Big Fish"

(*23 Running Words*)	errors	self-corrections
I got a fish! It was big and fast. Did you see my big fish? I will take it home and eat it.		
Totals:		

Running Words – Errors = % of Accuracy   23 – _____ = _____ % Accuracy
Running Words

Errors + Self-Corrections (S/C) = S/C Rate   _____ + _____ = 1 : ____ S/C Rate
Self-Corrections

Accuracy Levels
100% – 94% = easy
94% – 90% = instructional
below 90% = frustration

Comments and Observations:

Word List #11: Running Records

Name: _____   _____ % Accuracy

Date: _____   1: _____ S/C Ratio

"I Went to the Zoo"

(*41 Running Words*)	errors	self-corrections
I got to go to the zoo today. I got to take a ride on a giraffe. He was very big and fast. I said, "Take me for a ride giraffe!" He said, "Where do you want me to take you?"		
Totals:		

Running Words – Errors = % of Accuracy
Running Words

_41_ – _____ = _____ % Accuracy

Errors + Self-Corrections (S/C) = S/C Rate
Self-Corrections

_____ + _____ = _1 :___ S/C Rate

Accuracy Levels
100% – 94% = easy
94% – 90% = instructional
below 90% = frustration

Comments and Observations:

Word List	Times used in stories
1. over	3
2. made	3
3. came	3
4. of	5
5. been	3
6. many	4
7. were	2
8. us	5

Times Word Is Used in *Each* Story

	"The Farm"	"A Bath"	"Zoo Animals"	"Rain Puddles"
1. over	1	1	0	1
2. made	0	1	0	2
3. came	1	1	0	1
4. of	1	1	1	2
5. been	1	1	1	0
6. many	1	0	2	1
7. were	2	0	0	0
8. us	1	0	4	0

Number of times words from Word Lists #1–#11 are used → 85

Reading Strategies to Review

- Using Known Words
- Checking Pictures For Meaning
- Question Mark and Exclamation Point
- Suffixes ("s" and "ing" Endings)
- Quotation Marks (" ")
- Cross-Checking Initial Sounds with Meaning
- Comma
- Blending
- Wrap-Around Sentences

Word List #12: Sight-Word Stories

Story #1 — The Farm

Have you been to the farm?

On the farm you can see many animals.

When we were at the farm the cows came out of the barn and over to see us.

They were big!

(35 running words)

Story #2 — A Bath

I have been playing so I am going to take a bath.

I put water in the tub, but some of it came out of the tub and made it wet all over.

(33 running words)

Story #3 — Zoo Animals

Many of us have been to the zoo.

The zoo has many animals for us to see.

Do you want to come to the zoo with us?

Come with us to the zoo!

(33 running words)

Story #4 — Rain Puddles

It has been raining out today.

The rain came down out of the clouds and made many puddles.

I went out and jumped in all of the puddles.

Jumping in the puddles made me wet all over.

(37 running words)

Word List #12: Flash Cards

over	made
came	of
been	many
were	us

Word List #12: Homework

The Farm

Have you been to the farm?

On the farm you can see many animals.

When we were at the farm the cows came out of the barn and over to see us.

They were big!

A Bath

I have been playing so I am going to take a bath.

I put water in the tub, but some of it came out of the tub and made it wet all over.

Zoo Animals

Many of us have been to the zoo.

The zoo has many animals for us to see.

Do you want to come to the zoo with us?

Come with us to the zoo!

Rain Puddles

It has been raining out today.

The rain came down out of the clouds and made many puddles.

I went out and jumped in all of the puddles.

Jumping in the puddles made me wet all over.

Word List #12: Story Books

A Bath

I have been playing so I am going to take a bath.

I put water in the tub, but some of it came out of the tub and made it wet all over.

The Farm

Have you been to the farm?

On the farm you can see many animals.

When we were at the farm the cows came out of the barn and over to see us.

They were big!

Word List #12: Story Books

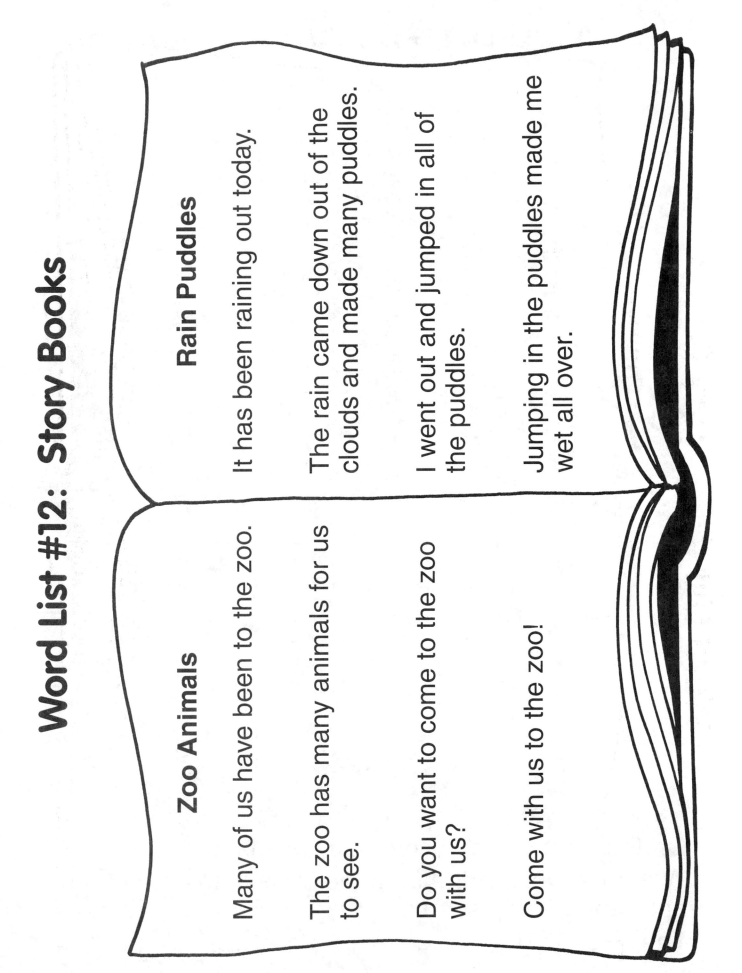

Zoo Animals

Many of us have been to the zoo.

The zoo has many animals for us to see.

Do you want to come to the zoo with us?

Come with us to the zoo!

Rain Puddles

It has been raining out today.

The rain came down out of the clouds and made many puddles.

I went out and jumped in all of the puddles.

Jumping in the puddles made me wet all over.

Word List #12: Library Box

The Farm

Have you been to the farm?

On the farm you can see many animals.

When we were at the farm the cows came out of the barn and over to see us.

They were big!

Word List #12: Library Box

A Bath

I have been playing so I am going to take a bath.
I put water in the tub, but some of it came out of the tub
and made it wet all over.

Word List #12: Library Box

Zoo Animals

Many of us have been to the zoo.
The zoo has many animals for us to see.
Do you want to come to the zoo with us?
Come with us to the zoo!

Word List #12: Library Box

Rain Puddles

It has been raining out today.

The rain came down out of the clouds and made many puddles.

I went out and jumped in all of the puddles.

Jumping in the puddles made me wet all over.

Word List #12: Cut-Up Sentences

It has been raining out today.

Have you been to the farm?

Come with us to the zoo!

Word List #12: Cut-Up Sentences

of	all	in	jumped	and	out	went	I
playing	been	have	I	puddles.	the
bath.	a	take	to	going	am	I	so

Word List #12: Running Records

Name: _____   _____ % Accuracy

Date: _____   1: _____ S/C Ratio

"Zoo Animals"

(33 Running Words)	errors	self-corrections
Many of us have been to the zoo. The zoo has many animals for us to see. Do you want to come to the zoo with us? Come with us to the zoo!		
Totals:		

Running Words – Errors = % of Accuracy
    Running Words

33 – _____ = _____ % Accuracy

Errors + Self-Corrections (S/C) = S/C Rate
    Self-Corrections

_____ + _____ = 1 : _____ S/C Rate

Accuracy Levels
100% – 94% = easy
94% – 90% = instructional
below 90% = frustration

Comments and Observations:

Word List #12: Running Records

Name: _____   _____ % Accuracy

Date: _____   1: _____ S/C Ratio

"Rain Puddles"

(33 Running Words)	errors	self-corrections
It has been raining out today. The rain came down out of the clouds and made many puddles. I went out and jumped in all of the puddles. Jumping in the puddles made me wet all over.		
Totals:		

Running Words – Errors = % of Accuracy   33 – _____ = _____ % Accuracy
    Running Words

Errors + Self-Corrections (S/C) = S/C Rate   _____ + _____ = 1 : ____ S/C Rate
    Self-Corrections

Accuracy Levels
100% – 94% = easy
94% – 90% = instructional
below 90% = frustration

Comments and Observations:

Sight-Word Index

Sight Word	Word List #	Sight Word	Word List #	Sight Word	Word List #
a	4	have	7	ride	11
after	7	he	4	run	6
all	9	help	5	said	5
am	7	here	3	saw	8
and	2	home	6	see	2
are	9	I	1	she	7
at	3	in	6	so	10
away	8	is	4	some	7
been	12	it	5	take	11
big	4	jump	3	tell	10
black	4	like	1	the	1
blue	1	little	5	they	9
boy	5	look	3	this	6
but	8	made	12	to	2
by	8	make	10	today	10
came	12	many	12	up	3
can	2	me	2	us	12
come	3	my	5	use	10
did	11	new	11	very	11
do	4	not	6	want	5
down	6	of	12	was	11
eat	8	on	5	we	2
fast	11	one	9	went	9
for	7	orange	1	were	12
friend	9	out	10	what	10
funny	6	over	12	when	8
get	7	play	2	where	9
go	2	please	7	will	3
good	9	purple	4	with	4
got	11	put	10	yellow	1
green	1	ran	8	yes	8
has	6	red	1	you	3